Copyright © 2018 Paul Deanno

All rights reserved. No part of this publication may be reproduced, distributed, or transmitted in any form or by any means, including photocopying, recording, or other electronic or mechanical methods, without the prior written permission of the publisher, except in the case of brief quotations embodied in critical reviews and certain other noncommercial uses permitted by copyright law. For permission requests, write to the publisher, addressed "Attention: Permissions Coordinator," at the address below.

ISBN: 978-1-7321173-2-7

Front cover image & book artwork by Toby Mikle.

First printing edition 2019.

Printed In China

Son & Reign Publishers
PO Box 2940
San Francisco, CA 94126

PaulDeannoBooks.com

Mommy, Mommy, did you know,
When a big storm comes, clouds grow and grow.
There's so much water above the ground,
Just ONE puffy cloud can weigh
TWO MILLION POUNDS!

It's silly for a zoo to be up that high,
But, Mommy, a cloud weighs as much
as **100 ELEPHANTS** in the sky!

Daddy, Daddy, when the ocean is warm,
We can find the world's **BIGGEST** storm.
Typhoon, cyclone, or hurricane,

Same huge storm... just with different names.
Winds can blow 100 miles an hour,

The ocean can rise 20 feet... Daddy, that's a
lot of **POWER!**

But did you know, Alaska has never been hit,
Because as soon as the ocean gets cold...

Hurricanes start to quit.

Inside the cloud, the floating ice is called **HAIL**,
And when it hits the ground, it leaves a slippery trail.

Even in summer, it can look like snow,
But, Nana, it's ice... and now you know!

Grandpa, Grandpa, I'd love for you to hear,
Summer is the hottest time of the year!
Every state has hit 100 degrees, that's true,
And all of them even hotter than that...

Except TWO.

FORECAST

84° S	80° S	83° M	87° T	84° W	85° Th	86° F

One is easy – Alaska – it's so high on the map,
But the other state, well, it's kind of a trap.
Maine, Vermont, North Dakota – NO!
It's actually a place where palm trees grow.
Grandpa, take a guess, give it a shot...
It's HAWAII, a place that's always warm...

But almost never hot.

Friends, Friends, it's beautiful to see,
Snow falling in my back yard so peacefully.
Everything covered in a blanket of white,
Flakes are still falling... What an amazing sight!

Sometimes I wonder, "How many snowflakes are there?"
It has to be **MILLIONS** dancing through the air.
Finding two alike would be a very hard game,
Did you know, in the **WHOLE WIDE WORLD**,
No two snowflakes are the same.
(That's right – EVERY one is different!)

Brother, Brother, here's what to do,
If a lightning storm is anywhere close to you.
Get inside – there's no time to wait,
The power with each lightning strike is great.
How hot is it? 50-THOUSAND DEGREES!
That's why it's not smart to just hide under
some trees.

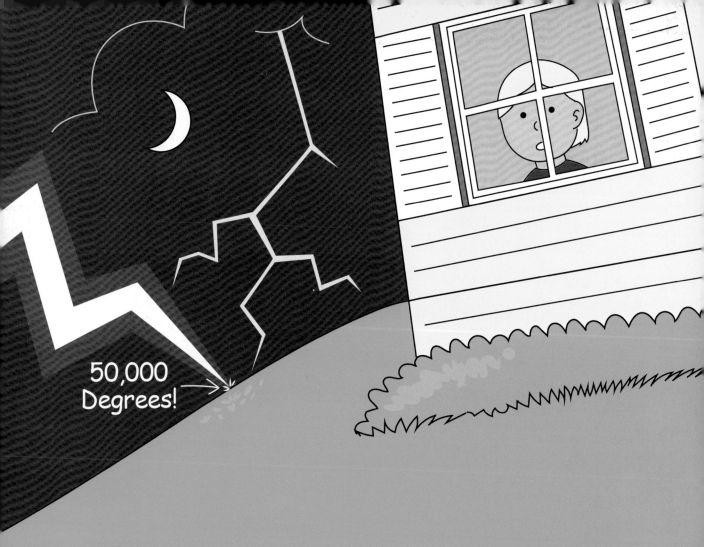

You see the "flash" first because light travels so fast,
And it's safe to go back outside after 30 minutes has passed.
Now Brother, this might make you think "No Way",
It's crazy but true – Lightning strikes Earth
8 MILLION TIMES EVERY DAY.

Uncle, Uncle, it's an amazing sight,

When two types of air take to the sky... and fight.
On one side, cold air, coming down from the north,
The other side is really warm – they'll battle back & forth.

Sometimes the fight will lead to a TWIST,
And that's when a TORNADO can't be missed.
The strongest winds on Earth can be found in its space,
And, Uncle, did you know, America gets MORE
TORNADOES than any other place?
(1200 a year to be exact.)

Teacher, Teacher, I think it's really neat,
That the closest star – the SUN – is our only source of heat.
Without it, the Earth would be a very cold place,
No wind, no weather, no Sun on my face.

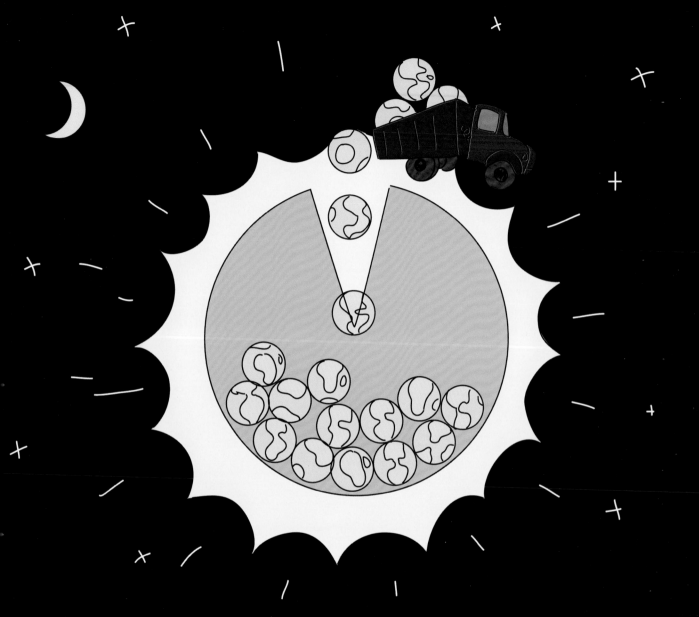

But did you know the Sun is super-tall & super-wide, Teacher, if you could open it up, more than **ONE MILLION EARTHS** would fit inside!

Did You Know?
It can SNOW in all 50 states,
even on Mauna Kea in Hawaii!

Did You Know?
The wind energy from just one hurricane
can power HALF of the Earth!

Weather!

Connect With Paul & "WOW! Weather"
On Social Media

f FACEBOOK -- WOW Weather
🐦 TWITTER -- @WowWeather_Book
🐦 TWITTER -- @PaulKPIX
📷 INSTAGRAM -- @BayAreaWxGuy

Other "WOW! Weather!" Titles

WOW! Weather!

To Read Paul's
"Weather 'Why's' For Kids" Blog,
Visit His Website:

PaulDeannoBooks.com

The End

About the Author

Paul Deanno has won four Emmy Awards for his work as a broadcast meteorologist in some of the largest television markets in the country. He is also the first meteorologist to do the weather on all three network morning newscasts: Good Morning America (ABC), The Today Show (NBC), and CBS This Morning. Paul lives in the San Francisco Bay Area with his beautiful wife, Suzanne, and their three boys.